In a World Where You Can Be Anything

Be...

Copyright © 2017 by Dawn Airhart Witte

Published by Dawn Airhart Witte

DesiretoInspireFoundation.org

Quantity sales. Special discounts are available on quantity purchases by corporations, associations and others. For details, contact the publisher: info@desiretoinspirefoundation.org.

Book Design and Illustrations
by Deborah Louise Brown

ISBN: 978-1-7320372-0-5

Second Edition

In a World Where You Can Be Anything

Be...

A Collection of Love with Friends to Inspire a Kindness Evolution

Dawn Airhart Witte

Foreword by Laura J. Swan, MA

Dedication

To all of my family and friends. You are all such beautiful gifts to me. Thank you for your love and support. You inspire me every single day and have all helped me to BE the person I am today.

Contents

BE...

Foreword

My reputation preceded me within the halls of my elementary school, but not because of any of the usual reasons a student becomes famous or infamous at such a young age. No, my claim to fame was Dawn Witte, my mother—the superstar.

My mom is one of the hardest working people I have ever met, and merely "doing everything" has never been enough to satisfy her. She volunteered in every classroom in which I was ever enrolled. The teachers loved her, and my fellow students absolutely adored her. I remember feeling slightly jealous of the fact that kids who were too cool to speak to me would cling to her throughout every lesson and follow her around like devoted puppies during break.

My mom volunteered in all my sister's classes, too, and eventually decided that simply spending her free time with a small percentage of students wasn't enough—she became PTA president, and a darn great one at that. Never merely content with the status quo, she overhauled old ways of thinking and made fantastic changes, including creating new fund-raisers and instating beneficial programs. Looking back, I'm pretty sure she actually did a lot more than her title gave her rein to do, but it didn't matter. People respected Dawn Witte, and when she suggested a change, they followed her lead.

I should probably point out that despite the fact that she basically made her role as PTA president into a full-time job, Mom never broke her stride as caretaker extraordinaire. Meanwhile, she was still raising a house full of rescued animals (at one point, we were sharing our small home with twelve cats, four dogs, and a varied assortment of small pet rodents as well), keeping that barn of a home clean, making us breakfast, packing lunches big enough to share with three friends, and crafting magnificent dinners to boot. Afternoons and weekends, she would dutifully take us to soccer practices, art classes, horseback riding lessons, gymnastics, piano instruction, or whatever hobby currently struck our fancy. For quite a few years, she and my father also coached our AYSO soccer teams. (Side note, my sister and I were terrible at all sports. But our parents cheered us on and coached our teams to victory many years in a row, despite having to claim ownership to two of the worst fumbling idiots on the field. If that's not the definition of a great parent, then I don't know what is.)

Mom never quite became a Girl Scout leader ("My idea of camping is staying in a motel," she'd joke to us after we'd come back feeling dirty and rugged from an overnight trip with the troop), but she was best friends with our troop leaders and helped out at every event that didn't involve braving the cold to sleep in a tent. To appease our grandmother—her mother-in-law—we ended up stretching our already overflowing schedule to join a chapter of National Charity League (NCL) over an hour away from our hometown. Mom warned us beforehand that pearls and balls and teas were not, well, her cup of tea, and that we were only doing this for Grandma's sake.

Of course, just try to take a guess as to who ended up becoming NCL president a few years into our tenure as members. Once again, the unstoppable Dawn Witte came in and made sweeping grand changes, instating more hands-on charity events and fund-raisers that took girls out of the parlor rooms and put us in real volunteer opportunities. That's my mom for you.

If I continued to list all my mother's various achievements and the mountain of volunteer work she continued to do after I went off to college, I would have to publish a new book to hold it all. She currently works with countless organizations that aid children, abused women, and animals. After struggling to find the best way to support her twin passions for charity work and small business, she was motivated to start her own company to unify the two and give back to her community. See? Somehow, doing everything is still never enough for her.

At the end of the day, my mom is simply one of the most compassionate, empathetic people I have ever met. She is genuinely good. I am so lucky to have been raised by a woman with both her heart and her ambition.

I've been abroad for the past year, but my friends still stop by my house to hang out with my mom. They tell her their problems, and she makes them dinner. A lot of my friends call her their "California Mom," their "Second Mom," or just "Mama Witte." There is so much more I could say about her, but for brevity's sake, I want to end this with just one more story.

One evening, with thousands of miles and many time zones separating us, I came home from a night out and video-called my mom. She answered, and I was obviously intoxicated and sobbing after a stupid fight with a boy I had cared about. Mom's reaction was calm: "Oh no, are you drunk? It's only 2:00 p.m. here. I've got things to get done." Then she sighed. "Hold on." She moved from the screen for a moment then returned . . . with a beer. Cracking it open, she took a swig and then looked back into the camera. "Okay, I'm ready. Tell me everything."

I love my mom.

Taylor Witte

When I was little and people would ask me what I wanted to be when I grew up, I would proudly say, "I want to be my mom." Well, my mom knew better, and she raised me to be myself—my own person. But there are traits of my mother that I do still wish to have. My mom has a passion for helping people and one of the biggest hearts I have ever known. When I was growing up, I told people I lived in a zoo because my mom could never turn away an orphaned animal.

We even brought a dog home all the way from Puerto Rico because she couldn't stand to leave him alone. I remember one day I got a text saying that we were going to foster two puppies until a rescue could find them a home. My first thought was "Oh yay, we are getting two new puppies" because I knew the second those two little dogs came into my house, my mom would never be able to let them go.

My mom's love doesn't only extend to animals. I was and am very grateful that child adoption is so difficult or else I am sure that I would have an infinite number of siblings. Even though my mom is only legally a mother of two, she is a maternal figure to so many more. She cannot help but extend that love that mothers give their children to anyone she meets that needs it. My mom has just this something extra about her that everyone sees but no one quite knows how to describe.

My friend likes to call it magical fairy powers, but I have also heard it described as an energy that just draws people to her. It is true. She does have this way about her, but I think it comes from her generous heart. Her goal in life is to help as many people as she can. Most everyone that knows her can say she has helped them in some way or another, even if it's just from bringing a good laugh or a smile. But my mom wants to help more than just the people she meets; she wants to extend this help to as many people as she can possibly reach.

This is one of the many reasons that I am proud to call her my mom. She has taught me that I can do anything that I set my mind to, and because of who she is, I have learned that I too want to help people. I know I am not the only person that has been inspired by my mom's love and generosity, and I know that little by little, this world can become a better place because of people like her.

Carrington Witte

Introduction

I love sharing books that have touched or inspired me. When I want to show my appreciation, celebrate a special occasion, or just say I was thinking about you and want to share these words with you, I look for books to express my gratitude and love. I want this book to bring a little inspiration to others. This book is the book I want to give to you. (Sorry, I have spoiled the surprise for everyone's Christmas presents this year.) Our words are so important. Actions may speak loudly, but so too do our words.

Words are magical. You never know the impact they can have on someone. We all have the power to make someone's day a little brighter or a little worse. I want my daughters to know this. I want to share these messages of love, courage, overcoming adversity, and giving kindness with everyone I can reach. The importance of these universal truths transcends time and space. I have witnessed the transformational power of my words and the words of others.

I have been told on a number of occasions that I have some sort of special energy—to which I usually scoff and laugh because the notion is funny. As much as I may dismiss it, I question what this "energy" or quality is that people believe I have. Here's what I have come up with: I do not think that I have a unique gift. I do see it as something special, but a power that everyone possesses should they choose. We are drawn to those who elevate and inspire us. People who see our beauty even when we don't see it in ourselves.

I will always help others when I am able; and sometimes, even when I am not able, I help anyway. Even if it is to give them a reason to smile or laugh. That is my calling. I think it is your calling. It is EVERYONE'S calling. Lift those around you. No matter your circumstances, you can always share kindness. Imagine a world where we all used our ability to make people feel good. We are all flawed in our own ways, but we are all special too. We can use our words to point out people's faults, because no one is perfect; or we can choose to use our words to change someone's day—or if we are really lucky, their life.

This book is just part of the legacy I wish to pass on to my daughters and others. Think of it as a little reference manual to help teach that little voice inside of their head and yours to be kind, strong, loving, inspired, genuine, happy, and grateful. For it is through living your life with those intentions that you will live the happiest and most fulfilling of lives.

I hope you enjoy my words; but more importantly, my wish is that my words will inspire you to live a life with as much love and as few regrets as possible.

Be ...

Genuine

gen · u · ine

/ˈjenyo͞oən/

Adjective

1. truly what something is said to be;
   authentic.
2. of a person, emotion, or action; sincere.

Authentic is important to BE in order for people to know the real YOU, but it is equally as important for you to be real with yourself. If you are able to love the person you are, then there should be no hesitation in showing who that is to the world. You are good enough. The right people will love exactly who you are, so there is no need to hide behind any facade. The people you want in your life will want to know your real self, not just an image you think they want you to be. Don't be afraid to ask a question you think sounds "dumb," because odds are that someone else has that same question. Own the things you know and the things you don't know. Own all of you: your quirks and your accomplishments.

It is okay to have vulnerabilities and weaknesses. We ALL do. You don't have to be perfect, but BE perfectly you. Have the confidence in yourself to be exactly who you are. When you trust in your own worth, you will be the best version of yourself. And you will have quality people in your life—because they will be drawn to the GENUINE you.

FIND YOUR GIFT AND THEN SHARE IT WITH THE WORLD WITHOUT HESITATION.

People's names matter. Make an effort to remember them.

Do NOT allow others to define you—ever. Define yourself (maybe with some input from those you love). Don't try to fit into a mold you think people want.

Life is often about compromise, but never compromise on character. Whether that character is yours or those you allow into your life.

Love yourself. You are amazing, and life feels really good when you like the person with whom you spend all of your time. I love you because you are lovable.

Do not think you know everything about anything. No one does because there is always more to learn. Be receptive to listening to those you oppose as well as those with whom you agree. Your life will be enriched by the knowledge you acquire on this journey.

Trust the vibes you get.
Energy does not lie.
—Mary Montalbo

NO ONE CAN BE YOU LIKE YOU!

Do not allow others to
define who you are.
Define yourself. It's
okay to not know
exactly who that is.
Life is a constant
learning process.

BE
GENUINE,
AUTHENTIC,
AND
REAL.

Extend the same
kindness and courtesy
to everyone you meet.
Be as kind and
respectful to the
person cleaning as
you would
the president.

Do not use the word
"promise" unless you fully intend
to stick by your words.
—Rory Airhart

OWN YOUR SHIT!

Do not say nothing
because you do not know
the right thing to say. If
it comes from your heart
and from a place of love, it
will be the right thing.

When you ask
someone how they are,
really want to learn
the answer.

No one is perfect. Choose your imperfections wisely.

There is a big difference between reasons and excuses.

Be as interested as much as you are interesting.

You may not be everyone's cup of tea, and that is OKAY. People who love chai tea really love chai tea.

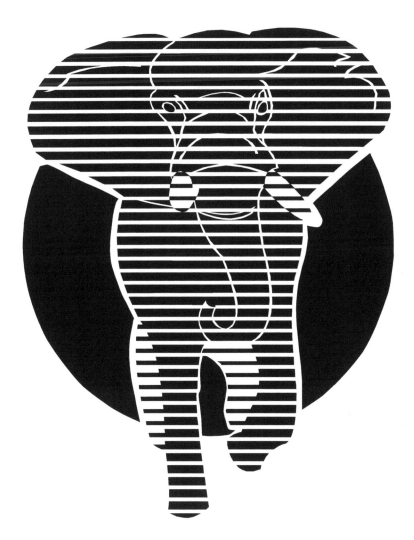

Tell the truth even when it's hard.

*Life is too short
to say things you
do not mean.*

Keep it real.

Loving

lov·ing
/ˈləv iNG/
adjective
   1. feeling or showing love or great care.

Love is the ultimate "BE" to BE because it is through LOVE that all things are possible. Without love, there is nothing of any importance or value. Love is what gives meaning to our lives, and it connects us here on earth and beyond. At the core of every great religion, great thinker, great leader, and great humanitarian, there is LOVE. I honor and respect everyone's religion or beliefs that come from a place of love. I do not care what political or religious label you put on yourself, where you are from, what color your skin is, what color your hair is, how much money you make, where you went to school, or whom you know. And the list goes on. None of that matters because LOVE is the ultimate Universal Truth. It is a feeling and concept that bridges all differences and EVERY soul can understand.

Learn to love unconditionally, like

dogs do, with their whole being.

When you love—and please do

 often—love with every

bit of your heart and soul.

It is the best way to love.

Be the friend you
wish you had. Be
the spouse, child,
neighbor, employee,
boss, partner,
patient, mother,
father, sister,
brother, auntie . . .

Do not fear death;
respect it. Treat each
day as a gift and
make sure those you
love know how loved
they are as often
as possible.

The same people who are
candy to our eyes may
be poison to our hearts.
Study their ingredients
before feeding them
to your soul.
—Mary Montalbo

Every

Soul

Matters.

34

Find your
passions and try
to explore those
as much as you
can in your life.

Surround yourself with love. When you are surrounded by family (pets included as well as children) and friends, you can get through any of life's challenges.

Dogs teach us

as much as

we teach them.

Do not be afraid to love with all that you have because love is amazing, even when it fails.

—Rory Airhart

Always make your decisions
from a place of love and
kindness. The decisions made
from other motives will never
have the best outcomes. Taking
the high road is sometimes
the more difficult path, but
it is always the right one.

If you don't believe in
soul mates, please do. You
will find many soul mates in
this lifetime. You will know
them when you find them.
Look for them everywhere,
including the animals we love.

People who are

worth your tears

won't make you cry.

Cherish those whom you love. Try to not let too much time go by without a visit, call, text, or e-mail.

Don't wait to write someone's tribute to tell the people you love how much they mean to you and what things you will always remember about them.

When you are writing their eulogy—which, sadly, you will have to do in this lifetime—don't let that be the only time you express it. Then it's too late.

Choose people on their character, not their quirks.

Love is the meaning of life.
Both giving and receiving
is what makes life
worth living.

You will never live a meaningful or fulfilling life if you only think of your own happiness. You truly have to live for others too!

Like everyone
you meet until
they give you a
reason not to.

Encouragement,
support, and love can
push people
to greatness.

THE MEANING
OF LIFE AS I
SEE IT? LOVE!
LOVE TRUMPS
ALL. NOTHING
EVEN COMES
CLOSE. THE END.

Next to love,
encouragement is
one of the greatest
gifts you can
give someone.

If what you get from your religion or belief system is hatred, you are doing it wrong.

Love travels everywhere.

Strong

strong
/strong/

adjective

1. having the power to move heavy weights or perform other physically demanding tasks
2. able to withstand great force or pressure

Being strong makes you resilient. Life will still have its challenges, but you will be able to endure the storms. It does not mean there are never moments of weakness. It means that we get up after each fall and take away the lesson every time. It means that we forgive ourselves and others to live happier lives. It means we find the courage to stand up for and help those who cannot do so for themselves. It means allowing ourselves to be human, imperfect. To feel and be messy and complicated beautiful beings who are able to overcome challenges. It means loving ourselves and others, even when it is hard. It means owning the responsibility that we are all role models for someone. You never know who is looking to you as an example of how to BE strong and keep going.

Be part of the

solution, not the

problem.

DO THE HARD
THINGS. YOU WILL BE
GLAD YOU DID WHEN
YOU COME OUT
STRONGER FOR IT.

You should ALWAYS be genuine, kind, and
compassionate. There is no compromise
on these values, or there shouldn't be.
There are many things to get righteously
angry about. When you get mad—and
please do when you must—let it be at
mean people, injustice, dishonesty. These
are abhorrent. Get mad. Get really, really
mad and then stand up. You are just as
bad as the bully if you do not stand up.
Standing up is the only thing that
changes the world.

We lead by example. We must.

Fill your life with those who will always have your back, and have theirs too.

There is no single
person who can fulfill
your every need.
Accept that some
people can be your
"fun to hang out with"
friend, but others are
fun AND will take
your 2:00 AM phone
call. Never lose the
"2 AMers."

When you are treated poorly by others, walk away, smile, and stay true to yourself. Don't ever let someone else's bitterness change the person you are.

You teach people how to treat you.

Never ask, "Why do these things happen to me?" Bad things, sad things, maddening things happen to everyone. No one is spared. Face each of life's challenges with as much love, kindness, and compassion as you are able. It will make you a stronger person.

Sometimes it is okay to
not be comfortable.
Stand up for what you
know is right, but do
not lecture others.

Strength does not come from what you can do; it comes from overcoming the things you once thought you could not do.

—Mary Montalbo

Try to avoid using the words
"always" and "never"
in arguments.

—Rory Airhart

Sometimes it is impossible,
but always strive to be gracious
and either apologize for not
being so or fight like hell to
justify why you were not.
This may require a reread.

If something in your life is not a source of happiness, change it.

There is a huge
difference between the
sad and the tragic. I
hope you are always
able to distinguish
between them.

Live fiercely.

Love with an open HEART.

Forgive when it's hard.

Avoid toxic people.

Let go of negativity.

Know when to say NO.

—Mary Montalbo

SOMETIMES
DOING THE RIGHT
THING IS
REALLY HARD,
BUT DO IT
ANYWAY.

The high road is always the right direction.

People can't give you what
they don't have.

—Dr. Phil

Give credit.
Don't take it.

Face your problems head-on.

—Mary Montalbo

Grateful

grate·ful

/grātfəl/

adjective

1. feeling or showing an appreciation of kindness; thankful.
2. received or experienced with gratitude; welcome.

If you are reading this, then you have much to be grateful for. You are alive, you can read, you have a book, you have time to read for pleasure, and so on. There are so many people in this world who envy what you have. You may not be exactly where you want to be in your life, but you have the opportunity every day to work towards getting to where you want to be. It is a gift to yourself to be grateful for what you DO have in your life. Look up to the sky, listen to the ocean, pet a puppy, feed the birds, hug a friend, tell your child you love them, and be grateful that you have these wonders in your life. Whether the glass is half full or half empty is irrelevant; when we see the fortune in having a glass at all, we will start seeing how full of blessings our lives really are.

You are deserving but never entitled. Know the difference between the two.

Always thank people as soon as possible for their kindness and generosity. The importance of showing your gratitude can't BE underestimated.

There is nothing in this
world that will bring you
more happiness and joy than
a sister or a daughter.
If you have both, you are
already luckier than most.
The right friends are sisters
too. Sons and brothers are
pretty fantastic too.

Say PLEASE and

THANK YOU much.

Appreciate all that you
have because there are so,
so many who would be
grateful to have but a
fraction of what you do.

Be grateful and always
show your gratitude for
even small gestures. A
smile and thank-you cost
nothing and require the
smallest of efforts.
Make it a reflex.

Your parents love you with all that
they are, no matter what. And
you are never too old to snuggle.

—Cathy Erskine

Never show up without bringing something.

We all have a need to be connected. Treat strangers like friends, and you will be surprised at what you will learn—about others and about yourself.

There are hundreds of opportunities every day to show gratitude and to count your blessings. Stay observant of these opportunities, and take advantage of them to make someone else's day. A smile, a thank-you note, just a quick text to someone that you were thinking of in that exact moment to tell them how much they mean to you . . . costs nothing. But the rewards are priceless.

—Kellee Everts

There will be transitional moments in your life that will never leave you. Make sure you fill those moments with things that matter and are filled with love.

EXPRESS YOUR PRAISE
AND APPRECIATION
MORE OFTEN THAN
YOUR CRITICISM.
AND WHEN
CRITICISM IS
NECESSARY, CONVEY
YOUR MESSAGE
WITH KINDNESS.

Inspired

In·spired

/in' spī(ə)rd/

adjective

1. of extraordinary quality, as if arising from some external creative impulse.
2. (of air or another substance) that is breathed in.

Wake up each and every day to look for the goodness and magic in the world. Be in awe of it. Celebrate it. Cheer for it. Albert Einstein said, "There are only two ways to live your life. One is as though nothing is a miracle. The other is as though everything is a miracle." His brilliance extends far beyond physics. There are no limits to inspiration. They say that necessity is the mother of all invention, but I believe that inspiration is even more important. Inspiration will create the drive to go out and make a difference in the world. It will be the motivation we need to accomplish great things for which we can take pride.

Just as we need to be inspired, we should also be aware that our actions can spark inspiration in someone else. You never know who is being inspired by your example. Set a good one.

Everyone brings
SOMETHING to the
table. Find that thing in
others as you find it within
yourself. Appreciate it
and cheer for it.

Dr. Seuss is

awesome.

Don't avoid doing
something just because
someone might
think it is crazy.

Clean your room.
Being surrounded by
order feels good.

Travel as much as you can. Experiences are far more valuable than things.

Create a list of things you want to experience in life and get out there and do them. Life goes by so quickly.
—Gayle Friedmann

No one knows everything, but please consider and do not dismiss insights from others. We are all learning as we go on this journey we call life.

Think outside of the "should box" as much as you can. Think about where our world would be if people never thought outside of the "should" box.

—Dre Seedarnee

Before anyone ever
became Successful, they
started with a dream.

Never say you can't . . .
always at least try.
As the saying goes,
better you try to fail
than fail to try.
—Rasheeda Seedarnee

EVERYONE you meet
will teach you something
about yourself.

*Surround yourself with people
who push you, who challenge you,
who make you laugh, who make
you better, who make you happy.*

—Mary Montalbo

Force yourself out of your comfort zone every once in a while. View the unknown as a new adventure. It may be difficult, but you will be happy you did.

Create your own opportunities.

Put your efforts into changing people's hearts rather than their minds.

Live in a world of infinite possibilities.

Kind

kind

/kīnd/

adjective

1. having or showing a friendly, generous, sympathetic, or warm-hearted nature.
2. agreeable or beneficial.

Do you want a kinder world? The world is a mirror that reflects what we put into it. Maybe one person can't change the entire world with their individual acts of kindness, but everyone can impact their world one act of kindness at a time. The effects of kindness can—and do—make ripples that reach far and wide. A smile, a laugh, a hug, a helping hand, or a word of encouragement costs absolutely nothing; but there is no price tag on the loving energy it creates in the world. The more you put out, the more you get back. Try it until it becomes a reflex.

You can help your friends make the little voice in their head a positive one. We never know what our words mean to someone. Hurtful or helpful. Which do you want to be remembered for?

Feed the birds.

And the bunnies,

and the gophers,

and the squirrels, etc.

Lift those around you . . . always. Being unkind or overly critical of others chips away, little by little, at YOUR heart. You will find that when you make others feel good about themselves it, in turn, makes you feel good about yourself.

Treat strangers with kindness. Ask a teller or customer service agent how they are doing. Give them a heartfelt compliment. Your little effort could be the brightest spot in an otherwise bad day.

Don't ever be so
consumed with
yourself that you
forget about those
around you.

Give to others when you can—and especially when you can't. You can always find someone whose needs are greater than yours.

Never make a decision
solely based on how
it affects you. Please
note the word "solely."
I want you to always
consider yourself, but
just know that your
decisions affect those
who love you.

Try to not say
things about
someone
that you
would not
say to them.

Try harder not to judge why a person does or does not do something. We do not know the journey they may be on or which may have just ended. This colors their world and guides their choices.

—Rory Airhart

Genuine compliments are a currency in and of themselves.

It is incumbent upon us to help others. Sometimes we are the others.

One person
can't help everyone,
but everyone
can help
someone.

**Apologies
should never
include "buts"
and "butts."**

ACTIONS MAY SPEAK
LOUDER THAN WORDS,
BUT WORDS ARE
POWERFUL. YOU CAN
GIVE SOMEONE A
CRITICISM OR A
COMPLIMENT.
CHOOSE THE
COMPLIMENT.

You can disagree without being disagreeable.

Happy

hap·py

/hapē/

adjective

1. feeling or showing pleasure or contentment. Cheerful, joyous, buoyant, pleased.
2. fortunate and convenient.

Happy just feels good. Joy can be contagious. When you are going through a difficult experience, finding the laughter or happiness may seem impossible; but I assure you it is not. Find the joy amidst the heartbreak. Shed the tears because that makes us real. Sometimes we must sit with the pain—because it means we loved. But don't stay there.

Do you want to be happy? Then project that. Sing, dance, paint, create, write, love, smile, laugh. Laugh so hard your stomach hurts and you can't breathe. Laughter is scientifically proven to produce endorphins. Endorphins are hormones secreted within the brain and nervous system which activate the body's opiate receptors. These cause an analgesic effect in our body, which makes us feel good. Fill your body with endorphins and release that happiness into the world. Make time to do the things that bring you happiness and remember to smile a lot. Everyone smiles in the same language. Your happiness will be a light for others.

Smile when you answer the phone; the person on the other end will feel it.

—Mary Montalbo

Laughter is timeless, imagination has no age, dreams are forever.

—Mary Montalbo

Everyone loves

a goofball.

Our special dog, Ethan, taught

us this special lesson.

Happiness is a choice. Everything else is a matter of perspective.

—Mary Montalbo

Sounds cliché, but the sooner you learn what is worth stressing about—and what is not worth stressing about—the happier you will be.

—Cathy Erskine

It's never too late
to start over. If you
are not happy with
yesterday, try something
different today.

—Mary Montalbo

Happiness really is a choice. You may not be happy all of the time, but make it the goal.

Always try to touch other's lives

with love and kindness whenever

you are able. You are always able.

**Try to find some kind
of joy even during the
darkest of times.**

When you are frustrated, remember to take a few moments to just BREATHE!

People and animals (SOULS) are like experiments. Watch what happens when you treat them with kindness, love, and laughter.

LIVE YOUR LIFE IN SUCH A WAY THAT WHEN YOU LOOK BACK OVER YOUR LIFE, YOU HAVE AS FEW REGRETS AS POSSIBLE.

Be

connected!

Laugh

Learn the names of
every plant and
animal you can and
notice and
appreciate them
when you see them.

No matter which path you choose

in life, know there will be forks,

hills, and obstacles. Go over,

around, under, or through them.

Don't let them stand in your way.

Smile

FACES ON
BANANAS
ARE FUNNY.
BARBIE
CLOTHES
AND
GOOGLY
EYES ARE
TOO.

It's okay to cry. Just try to make your laughter outweigh your tears.

Find the things in life
that you love most.
Surround yourself
with them. I hope they
are the right things.

There are a limited number of hours in the day and days in a lifetime. Try spending most of your energy focusing on being constructive, efficient, and positive.

Happiness was defined by the
ancient Greeks as the joy we
feel in striving to live up to
our potential.

Soul mates DO
exist.

The End

Afterword

Dawn Witte is a rare type of human being who gives with her whole heart and holds nothing back. She was born to love, and loving is what she does best. When she has given all the love she has inside, she suddenly sources more and more to keep on giving, and finds more and more ways to help others. The book you hold now is but one of her many expressions of her love for humanity, and is but one of her many efforts to make this world a more beautiful place. And this is what truly makes her happy... because there is nothing quite as fulfilling as giving back and serving others with all our hearts.

And this book couldn't have come at a better time in human history. Humanity is going through challenges on many levels: economically, environmentally, emotionally, socially, and financially... and many more. Everywhere we turn there are reasons to feel discouraged or depressed about the state of our world. And this can be overwhelming if we allow it to be all that we see.

But there are also equally as many reasons, should we choose to see them, to be happy and feel love in our hearts every day. A hug from a loved one. A beautiful sunset. The sound of the birds chirping, or a smile from a child. Beauty surrounds us every day, but we have to choose to see it and feel it in each moment. The core message of "Be" is that we all have a choice about *who we want to be*, and how we want to feel, no matter what is going on around us in the world. And who we choose to be has a profound ripple effect on the world around us.

Life can be full of obstacles and challenges, but the bottom line is that we always have a choice. Do we want to live a life of gratitude and love, or one of fear and discouragement? Do we want to share hope and inspiration, or do we want to spread negativity and judgment? The simple choices we make around these very questions affect us deeply, and they affect the quality of our lives in every moment of every day.

"Be" invites us all to see a world through the eyes of love, and to elevate our consciousness to a higher place so we can live a life most aligned with our hearts. Through simple, easily accessible messages, each chapter opens our hearts more and more to the profound importance of kindness and giving in our lives. And the world needs this encouragement and inspiration now more than ever before.

When Dawn asked me if I would write the afterword for this book you hold right now, I was in the throes of finishing my own book (two of them actually) and was about to give birth to my son at any moment. My son ended up coming three weeks early, and this further amplified my workload and busy schedule. It could not have been a more busy time of my life, and I was saying no to almost every request that came my way.

But when I received the request from Dawn to write the words I share with you now, I felt an enthusiastic, unquestionable, undeniable YES reverberate through my whole body. There was no question in my mind… I could not be more honored to do it. Because I want with every fiber of my being for as many people as possible to receive the messages of this book. I hope that you feel the simple yet life changing wisdom that is offered here, and that you create a better life because of it. I know how much the world needs the wisdom and love that she shares here, and I'm so very grateful you're holding a copy of this book right here and now.

I have no doubt that humanity is heading in the right direction because people like Dawn Witte are in the world. She is a bright light that shines in all directions, and all who are in her presence feel the power of her giving heart. From helping feed and care for the children of Africa, to supporting her girlfriends in need, to serving as the PTA president, to founding inspirational nonprofits, to fostering numerous rescue animals, to being the very best mother you could ever imagine... Dawn Witte shares her heart fully in all that she does. She walks her talk, and she lives as love in all that she does. She lives and breathes the messages of this book every day, and that's what makes it such a deeply authentic and beautiful work of art.

This book is her way of sharing her heart with you. I trust you will feel like a more positive, happy person through reading it... just as I did.

With Love,
Laura
xo

Laura J. Swan, MA is a women's transformational coach, author, and leadership mentor. She has worked with women and girls for over 20 years. LauraJSwan.com

160

Next Steps

"In a world where you can BE anything ..." That's how this book starts out and that's how we move forward on a journey to BE the change in the world that makes our hearts sing. You have your journey and I have mine ~ maybe we can travel together for awhile.

Part of my journey includes trips to Africa. Join me at **DesiretoInspireFoundation.org** to learn more about life-changing projects and special children I have met. These beautiful children are yearning to be educated, fed, clothed, loved and encouraged on their own journeys.

Learn how you can help provide clean water, books, education, and love to children all over the world. The change we wish to see in the world is ours to BE. Perhaps we can't completely eliminate poverty and hunger in the world but we surely can end it for those whose lives we know. As Margaret Mead so beautifully stated, "Never doubt that a small group of thoughtful, committed, citizens can change the world. Indeed, it is the only thing that ever has."

Artist—Linda Marie Fabry

Linda Marie Fabry is a contemporary American visionary artist. Since the introduction of her acrylic on canvas paintings to the online marketplace in 2001, her work has been collected by thousands of individuals and corporations throughout the world. She has received numerous awards, including Best of Show from a PBS televised exhibition in Redding, California.

A diverse artist, Ms. Fabry has worked with a variety of media, including acrylics, watercolor, pastel, ceramic, and mixed media. She has completed several public works in both Illinois and Wisconsin. One of her pieces, a functional sculpture commissioned in 2005 by the Indian Trails Public Library in Wheeling, Illinois, was recognized and catalogued by the Smithsonian American Arts Museum.

In May of 2010, Linda graduated magna cum laude with a bachelor's degree in art therapy from Marian University in Fond du Lac, Wisconsin, where she was the recipient of several awards for academic performance and community involvement.

During her undergraduate studies, while pursuing a theology minor, Linda became interested in transpersonal psychology and the spiritual aspect of healing. She is trained in Healing Touch and incorporates knowledge of metaphysics into her work.

In addition to her work as a fine artist, Linda is an expressive arts facilitator, sharing the healing benefits of creative expression with others through workshops and individual coaching.

About the Author

Dawn Airhart Witte is the founder of the Desire to Inspire Foundation and co-founder of I Give On: The Givers Marketplace.

Being a mom is her proudest role and title. Because of her great love for children she started the Desire to Inspire Foundation which provides children around the world with a mother's love and care. A philanthropist from an early age, Dawn's company, I Give On, began with her passion for fundraising and the nonprofit sector, while supporting businesses who generously donate to worthy causes. Her steadfast resolve in eradicating hunger and poverty is one of her greatest driving forces.

Her lifelong appreciation for community involvement earned her the honor of the Glendale News Press's "One of the 103 Most Influential People in the Foothills." Dawn served two terms as Public Works Commissioner for the City of La Canada Flintridge, and two terms as President of the National Charity League - Los Angeles Founder Chapter (NCL-LA). Raising her daughters, Taylor and Carrington, is her proudest accomplishment.

Please follow her journey as she continues to touch lives all over the world.

Visit DesiretoInspireFoundation.org and www.IGiveOn.com.

Hope & Love

Notes

Made in the USA
San Bernardino, CA
01 February 2019